In the name of God, most Gracious, most Merciful

THE ISLAMIC WILL

A Practical Guide to Being Prepared for Death and Writing your Will according to the *Shari'a* of Islam and English Law

**Hajj 'Abdal-Haqq
and 'A'isha Bewley
and
Ahmad Thomson**

Published in Great Britain by:

Dar Al Taqwa Ltd
7A Melcombe Street
Baker Street
London NW1 6AE

Tel: 0171-935-6385
Fax: 0171-224-3894

Edited by: Dr. Muhammad Isa Waley

Typesetting by: Ahmad Thomson

Printed in Great Britain by:

Deluxe Printers
245A Acton Lane
Park Royal
London NW10 7NR

Tel: 0181-965-1771

Contents

Part 1 – Preparing for Death

*(Part 1 was written principally by
Hajj 'Abdal-Haqq and 'A'isha Bewley)*

Part 2 – Writing your Will

*(Part 2 was written principally by
Ahmad Thomson)*

Part 1

Preparing for Death

Preface

"Every self will taste death." In this clear *aya* (3.185, 21.35 and 29.57) Allah informs us of the inevitability of our own death and that of every single human being. Death is in fact, ironically, the only certain fact of life. In spite of this, the dominant *kafir* culture, which invests everything in the life of this world, has turned the subject of death into a taboo, something to be avoided at all costs. Everything is geared towards having us believe that this life goes on forever. Death, if it takes place, is something that only happens to other people. And anyway a cure for death may be just over the horizon! Death has become the domain of specialists who are paid to make sure that it infringes as little as possible on the ongoing life of those connected with it. The idea of preparing sensibly for one's own death or of dealing in a practical way with the death of those who are close to us is now considered morbid to the point of gruesomeness.

However, as is the case with everything in our lives, the matter of death and dying has been covered in detail by Allah and His Messenger, may Allah bless him and grant him peace, and the guidance of Islam is available to us to show us how to deal with every aspect of it. It is absolutely vital for every Muslim, especially those of us who live in *kafir* lands, to know about this matter so that we will be able to prepare ourselves, inwardly and outwardly, for our own approaching death and also so that we will know exactly what to do when those near and dear to us die. This is an obligatory aspect of our *deen* and one that we cannot allow to be taken out of our hands. There is no area in which the pleasure of Allah and His Messenger could be more important. It is hoped that this small book will provide all the practical information needed to enable Muslims in this country to make the necessary preparations for their own death and also to take all the necessary steps when those who are close to them reach the end of their lives in this world.

At the Deathbed

The state of mind of a person at the door of death is of paramount importance. It is vital that their fear of what is coming and also of the effects of any wrong actions they may have committed during their lives should be balanced by an equally vibrant hope in the mercy of Allah. Allah Almighty says:

"O My slaves who have been profligate against yourselves, do not despair of the mercy of Allah. Allah forgives all wrong actions. He is the Forgiving, the Merciful." (39.50)

The Prophet, may Allah bless him and grant him peace, said: "Let none of you die except with good thoughts of Allah, the Mighty and Exalted." And there is another *Hadith* which says: The Prophet once visited a man who was dying and asked him, "How do you feel?" He answered, "I have hope in Allah, O Messenger of Allah, and I also fear as to the consequences of my sins." The Prophet said, "Whenever these two are combined in the heart of a believer in a situation like this, Allah grants him what he hopes for and shields him from what he fears." The Messenger of Allah, may Allah bless him and grant him peace, also said: "Allah, the Blessed and Exalted said, 'If My slave longs to meet Me, I long to meet him, but if he is averse to meeting Me then I am averse to meeting him.'"

Therefore people close to death should feel optimistic about the outcome of their forthcoming meeting with their Lord and if those who are with them sense that this is not the case they should remind them that Allah loves to forgive the wrong actions of His slaves and that His mercy is much greater than His wrath.

The *shahada* should be repeated in the presence of the dying so that they will be reminded of it and if possible make it the last thing they say. It is also generally considered good to recite *Surat YaSin* in the presence of people who are dying and that this will ease for them the path to death.

> The Prophet, may Allah bless him and grant him peace, said: "Repeat, 'There is no god but Allah' to your dying people so that they may hear and repeat it." And he also said: "He is destined for Paradise whose last words in life are: 'There is no god but Allah'." He further said: "Recite *YaSin* to the dying." And also: "The heart of the Qur'an is *YaSin*. Whenever a person recites it, seeking Allah and the Hereafter, Allah forgives them. Recite it for your dying." And again: "If *YaSin* is recited for a dying person, Allah makes matters easier for him."

After the person has died their eyes should be closed and if possible their body should be turned towards the *qibla*. Those present should make *du'a* for the dead person asking Allah to ease the passage from life to death for them and to strengthen them when the angels question them and to grant them His forgiveness and mercy.

> The Prophet, may Allah bless him and grant him peace, visited Abu Salama after he died and found him lying with his eyes open. He closed his eyes, saying, "When the soul departs, sight follows it." He

said on another occasion, "When you visit a dead person, close his eyes. Sight follows the soul as it departs. And make supplication for good things: the angels pray with you for the acceptance of your supplication."

There is, of course, no harm in weeping and natural grief when someone dies although self-control and patience are better if that is possible. However, crying out and shouting and wailing and other excessive demonstrations of grief are forbidden.

Preparing the Dead for Burial

The washing and shrouding of the dead for burial is according to some a *fard kifaya* - an obligatory duty that must be fulfilled by someone. It is at the very least an important *Sunna*. In any case it is something that is owed to the honour and dignity of every Muslim when they leave this world. No one will pretend that it is a pleasant duty to have to perform but nor is it in any way distasteful or abhorrent although it increasingly now seems to be seen in that light. It should be seen for the normal, necessary and important human duty which it in fact is. There are, of course, in every Muslim community people who have taken it on themselves to prepare the dead for burial and there is no reason why their services should not be engaged. However, it is very important that every Muslim should be able to undertake this task if necessary and therefore the steps to be taken after someone dies should form part of the basic knowledge of every Muslim man and woman.

Once it is certain that a person is dead it is important that their body should be prepared and buried in the shortest practical time, although there is no harm in transporting the deceased from one land to another if he or she has not been buried and if this appears to be really necessary.

The Prophet, may Allah bless him and grant him peace, said: "Make haste. The body of a Muslim should not be kept among his family." He further said: "When one of your family dies, do not detain him. Speed him to his grave." And again: "Make haste with the dead body. If its owner was righteous, you are forwarding it to what is better. If the case was otherwise, then you are freeing your necks of an evil burden."

Firstly it is recommended to bind the jaws with a wide cloth tied at the top of the head and to gently straighten the joints. Any clothes should be removed and the body covered with a cloth to protect it from being seen. It is also recommended to inform people by means of a simple public announcement that the death has taken place so that people will be ready to attend the funeral.

Washing the body

All Muslims should be washed prior to their shrouding and burial. The only exceptions are the bodies of Muslims killed fighting in the way of Allah on the battlefield, when their bodies should be buried directly, exactly as they are; and the bodies of those who are badly mutilated, as in an accident or in a fire, in which case *tayammum* is done on the body instead of washing; and also babies which are miscarried or stillborn with no observable signs of life, in which case no rites of any sort, including washing, shrouding and the funeral prayer, are carried out. If no water is available then *tayammum* should be done on the body.

The basic rule for those who do the washing is that men wash men and women wash women. It is, however, generally considered appropriate for a man to wash his wife and a wife her husband. It is also permitted for a man to wash female relatives whom he would have been barred from marrying, although in this case the body should be washed through a covering cloth. There is no harm in women washing the body of a young boy of six or seven years old, but men should not wash the bodies of young girls.

When a woman dies and there are no women to wash her, and no husband, and no man related to her who would have been barred from marrying her while she was alive, then she should be purified by *tayammum*, that is, by wiping her face and hands with earth. Similarly, when a man dies and there are no men to wash him, and no wife, and no woman related to him whom she would have been barred from marrying while he was alive, then he should be purified by *tayyamum*, that is, by wiping his face and hands and arms up to the elbows with earth.

It is in any case unlawful to look directly at the private parts of the dead person which should be kept covered at all times. Nor should the private parts be touched directly: they should be washed with a cloth wrapped round the hand. The nails should not be cut nor should hair be trimmed or shaved off.

The body should be placed on a raised trestle or something similar to make the washing easier and so that the water runs off. It is easier to wash the body before *rigor mortis* (the stiffening of the body which takes place within twenty-four hours of death, and which may last for several days) occurs.

Firstly the stomach should be gently squeezed so that any excess fecal matter may be expelled and removed. Then the private parts should be washed without being exposed. Then *wudu'* should be done on the body, as for the prayer.

Then the whole body should be washed as when doing *ghusl* for *janaba*: starting with the head and then the top half of the body, right then left, followed by the legs, right then left. This should be done an odd number of times and in the final washing the water should be perfumed, it being recommended to use camphor for this purpose. It is also recommended to put perfume on the places which touch the ground during *sajda*, in other words the forehead, nose, palms, knees and toes.

Shrouding the Body

After it has been washed the body should be dried and shrouded. This entails wrapping the body completely in an odd number of lengths of cloth which should preferably be white. It is said that the minimum number of these should be three and the maximum seven. It is good to block the nostrils, ears and eyes with cotton before wrapping, and to bind the feet and hands together. There is no harm in making one of the cloths a turban for the head nor in using simple garments such as long shirts or waist wrappers, in which case each garment counts as one piece of cloth. The wrapping should be made as secure as possible to prevent any possibility of it unravelling and the body becoming exposed when being moved. The Prophet, may Allah bless him and grant him peace, was shrouded in three lengths of fine white cotton cloth, none of which was a shirt or turban, each layer being well wrapped round him.

The Prophet, may Allah bless him and grant him peace, said: "Wear white clothes. They are best for you. And choose them for shrouding your dead." He also said: "Do not be extravagant where the shroud is concerned. It soon falls away."

After this the best thing is for the body to be laid directly onto the bier to be placed straight into the grave. However, to comply with the law in England and Wales it may be necessary to put the body in a coffin prior to burial and in this case the simplest possible one should be used. The body or coffin should then be covered with a simple drape in readiness for the funeral prayer.

Whoever washes and shrouds the body should not mention anything unpleasant about it, such as smell or appearance, to others afterwards. It has been related from Abu Rafi' Aslam that the Messenger of Allah, may Allah bless him and grant him peace, said, "Anyone who washes a dead person and keeps quiet about him, Allah will forgive him forty times."

It is preferable but not obligatory that whoever washes and shrouds the body should then have a *ghusl*.

The Funeral Procession

Although the body can be first taken to the mosque and the funeral prayer done there, it is more usual for the body to be taken to the graveside, where the funeral prayer is done immediately before the body is buried. Whoever is on foot should walk ahead of the bier, whoever is riding should follow behind it, and the women – preferably only close female relatives should attend – should follow behind the men. It is also said that everyone should follow behind the bier. Incense should not be burned during funeral processions, nor should flaming torches be carried.

It has been related from Abu Hurayra that the Messenger of Allah, may Allah bless him and grant him peace, said, "Carry the bier quickly. If the dead person was righteous, it is good you are advancing him to. If he was other than that, then it is an evil you are removing from your necks." And it has been related from Abu Sa'id al-Khudri that the Prophet said, "When a body is laid out and the men carry it on their shoulders, if its owner was righteous, it says, 'Take me forward,' and if its owner was not righteous, it says, 'Woe to me, where are you taking it?' Everything except man hears its voice. If anyone were to hear it, he would faint."

It has been related by 'Ali ibn Abi Talib that the Prophet, may Allah bless him and grant him peace, used to stand up when a funeral procession passed by, and then sit down again afterwards – although it is also said that this has been abrogated.

The bier is placed between the grave and the *Imam* during the funeral prayer, and is buried once the prayer has been completed.

The Funeral Prayer

The funeral prayer is only said over dead Muslims, in their presence, not in their absence, although if a body has already been buried, without the funeral prayer having been done and the grave has already been filled in, then it is still permissible to do the funeral prayer at the graveside, provided that the funeral prayer has not already been done for the deceased by others. You do not do the funeral prayer a second time if it has already been done once. The funeral prayer is to be done for a person as long as most of the body remains intact and has not been destroyed or is missing. If the father is a Muslim, then his children are regarded as Muslim, but if only the mother is a Muslim, they are not.

The following do not have the funeral prayer said over them: martyrs killed on the battlefield while fighting in the way of Allah, stillborn babies and miscarried foetuses. This also applies if most of the body has been destroyed or is missing: where, for example, only someone's hand or foot remains. This also applies, but for different reasons, to burying *kafirun* or other non-Muslims if this is necessary. There is no harm, for example, in simply burying *kafir* relatives.

If a Muslim commits suicide, the funeral prayer is still done for him. The funeral prayer is also done for any Muslim killed by the *Imam* as a *hadd* punishment, or because they have killed someone, although the *Imam* himself should not participate in the prayer for him. Someone else should lead the prayer. The funeral prayer is also done for a child born out of wedlock and for its parents.

There is no harm in having one funeral prayer for several dead people, although the funeral prayer can be done for each of them in turn. If there are both men and women among the dead, the men are placed nearest to the *Imam*. If there are only men, the best of them is placed nearest to the *Imam*. If there are women and children as well, they are placed behind the men in the direction of the *qibla*. There is no harm in a number of bodies being placed in a row, in which case the one nearest the *Imam* should be the best of them. The body nearest to the *Imam* should be the most virtuous, and men are ahead of women, and free people ahead of slaves, and the old of each class before the young, and the one who has distinction in the *deen* is put in front. If they are equal, then advancement is by age, and if they are still equal, then it is by lots or mutual agreement. If a number of people are being buried in one grave, the best should be nearest the *qibla*.

There is a great reward to be gained from doing the prayer and for being present at the burial. This reward is equivalent in size to Mount Uhud (Bukhari and Muslim).

The form of the prayer, which is performed standing and facing the *qibla*, is simple, but its content is not fixed. It is done standing in rows, with the men in front of the women. Anyone doing the funeral prayer should fulfil all the requirements for the prayer in general, including being in *wudu'* and making the *niyya* for the prayer. However, the funeral prayer can be done between *'asr* and *maghrib*, and between *subh* and *shuruq*, even if *'asr* or *subh* have already been prayed at their times.

The funeral prayer has four pillars: intention, the four *takbirs*, the supplication for the deceased, and the *salam*. Some add that the *Fatiha* can be recited after the first *takbir*.

The *Imam*, who stands opposite the chest if the deceased is a man and opposite the waist if the deceased is a woman, raises his hands in the first *takbir*, but need not raise them in the remaining *takbirs*, although there is no harm in doing so. Those praying behind the *Imam* should do as he does.

The most complete form in the supplication is to begin with praising Allah, then the prayer on the Messenger of Allah, may Allah bless him and grant him peace, and then supplication for the deceased. If you like you can make a *du'a* after the fourth *takbir* before the *salam* or if you like, you can say the *salam* directly after the *takbir*.

There is no specific formula for the *du'a* to be made when doing the funeral prayer. Whatever has been reliably transmitted concerning it is acceptable.

It has been related that Abu Hurayra was asked, "How do you pray over the dead?" and Abu Hurayra replied, "By the Life of Allah, I will tell you! I follow with the family and when the corpse is put down I say, 'Allah is greater' and praise Allah and ask for blessings on his Prophet. Then I say, 'O Allah, he is Your slave and the son of Your male slave and Your female slave. He used to testify that there is no god but You and that Muhammad is Your slave and Your Messenger, and You know that best. O Allah, if he acted well, then increase for him his good action, and if he acted wrongly, then overlook his wrong actions. O Allah, do not deprive us of his reward, and do not try us after him.'"

'Allahumma innahu 'abduka wa' bnu 'abdika wa' bnu amatika. Kana yashhadu an la ilaha illa ant wa anna Muhammadan 'abduka wa rasooluka, wa Anta a'lamu bihi. Allahumma in kana muhsinan fa-zid fi ihsanihi, wa in kana musiyan fa-tajawaz an sayyi'atihi. Allahumma la tahrimna ajrahu wa la taftina ba'dahu.'

One good thing to say after doing the *takbir* is:

"Praise be to Allah Who makes to die and brings to life, and praise be to Allah Who brings the dead to life. To Him belong Greatness, Sovereignty, Power, Exaltedness, and He has power over all things. O Allah, bless Muhammad and the family of Muhammad as You blessed and were merciful to and poured goodness on Ibrahim and the family of Ibrahim. In all the worlds, You are Praiseworthy, Glorious. O Allah, he is Your slave and the son of Your slaves. You created him and provided for him. You made him die and You will bring him back to life and You know best about his outward and his inward. We have come to You as intercessors on his behalf so please accept our intercession. O Allah, we seek safety for him by Your bond of protection with him. Certainly You keep Your word and promise. O Allah, protect him from the trials of the grave and from the torment of Hell. O Allah, forgive him, have mercy on him, pardon him and grant him well-being. Be generous to him when he arrives and open the way wide for him to come in. Wash him with water, snow and ice and cleanse him from his wrong actions as a white garment is cleansed of dirt. Give him a home better than the home he had, a family better than the family he had and a wife better than the wife he had. O Allah, if he was right-acting, increase him in his right actions and if he was wrongdoing, then overlook his wrong actions. O Allah, he has come to You and You are the Best to whom anyone can come. He is in need of Your mercy and You have no need to punish him. O Allah, make his speech firm when he is questioned and do not test him in his grave beyond what he can bear. Do not deprive us of our reward for doing this on his behalf and do not test us after him."

(As with all these *du'as*, if the dead person is a woman then you say: "O Allah, she is Your slave and the daughter of Your slaves..." and you go on making the object of the *du'a* feminine rather than masculine. The only difference is that you do not say, "Give her a husband better than her husband..." because in the Garden she can be the wife of the man who was her husband in this world and the women of the Garden are attached only to their husbands and have no desire for anyone else. A man may have many wives in the Garden whereas women only have one husband.)

You say this after each *takbir* and then after the fourth *takbir* you say:

"O Allah, forgive those who are alive and those who are dead, those who are present with us and those who are absent, those who are young and those who are old, those who are male and those who are female. You know everything that we do and where we will end up – and forgive our parents and those who have gone before us with *iman* and all the Muslims both men and women and all the *mu'minun* both men and women, the living and the dead. O Allah, as for whomever of us You keep alive, keep him alive in *iman,* and as for whomever You take back to Yourself, take him back as a Muslim. Make us glad when we meet You. Make us pleasing at the time of our death and make death pleasant for us. Make it a source of rest and happiness for us."

After this you say the *salam.*

If the dead person is a child, you can make your *du'a* in this way: First you praise Allah *tabaraka wa ta'ala* and ask for blessings on His Prophet Muhammad, may Allah bless him and grant him peace, and then you say:

"O Allah, he is Your slave and the son of Your slaves. You created him and provided for him. You made him die and will bring him to life. Make him a forerunner and a stored-up treasure and a reward for his parents. Make their balances heavy through him and make their reward greater because of him and do not deprive either us or them of their reward through him and do not test either us or them after him. O Allah, give him the company of the right-acting *mu'minun* who have gone ahead and place him under the guardianship of Ibrahim. Give him a house better than the one he had and a family better than the one he had. Save him from the trial of the grave and the torment of Hell."

You say this after each *takbir* and after the fourth you say:

"O Allah, forgive our forebears and predecessors and those who have gone before us. O Allah, whomever among us You keep alive make him live in *iman,* and whomever You take back to Yourself take him back as a Muslim. Forgive all the Muslims both men and women and all the *mu'minun* both men and women, the living and the dead."

Then you say the *salam.*

Some Muslims recite the *Fatiha* after the first *takbir*, a prayer on the Prophet after the second *takbir*, a supplication for the deceased after the third *takbir*, and nothing after the fourth *takbir*, which is followed almost immediately by the *salam.* As already stated, there is no specific formula for the *du'a* to be made when doing the funeral prayer. Whatever has been reliably transmitted concerning it is acceptable.

The Burial

There are two types of grave: the *lahd* and the *shaqq.* The *shaqq* is a simple trench. The *lahd* is one in which, after you have dug the basic trench, you dig out a niche for the body at the bottom of the side which faces *qibla* so that the body is protected by the overhang. This should be done provided that the earth is firm enough and will not crumble or cave in. This was how the grave of the Prophet was dug, may Allah bless him and grant him peace.

There is no harm in burying a dead person facing in any direction, although it is better to bury a person facing the *qibla.* The dead body should be placed in the grave by as many men as are needed to do so. If the deceased is a woman, then her husband should hold the body from underneath and her male relatives from above her. If there are no righteous male believers, and if there are women who can bury her, then this is better than having non-relatives bury her.

The Prophet Muhammad, may Allah bless him and grant him peace, said, "When you lower your dead into their graves, say, 'In the Name of Allah, the Merciful, the Compassionate.'"

The dead person should be placed on his right side, facing the *qibla*, and the ties of the shrouds loosened at his head and feet. If the body is not in a coffin – which is not required by the *Shari'a*, but which is sometimes imposed by present-day local authorities – the head and feet can be supported with loose earth, and some kind of protective covering, such as slabs made of clay and straw, or a wooden board, can be placed directly over or against the back of the body, depending on which type of grave has been dug. If a coffin is being used, then there is no need for any additional protective covering.

It is recommended to make supplication for the dead person at this point, before the body is covered with earth, and it is recommended that all those who are present – or, if there is a large number of people present, then those who are near – should throw a few (at least three) handfuls of earth into the grave when it is being filled in.

When this is done, you should say:

> "O Allah, our companion is now with You. He has left this world behind him and is in need of what is with You. O Allah, make his speech firm when he is questioned and do not test him in his grave beyond what he can bear. Grant that he may be in the company of the Prophet Muhammad, may Allah bless him and grant him peace."

The Prophet Muhammad, may Allah bless him and
grant him peace, used to stand at the grave of a Muslim who had just been buried and say, "Ask Allah's
forgiveness for your brother, and ask Allah to grant
him perseverance – he is being questioned."

There is no harm in reciting *Surat YaSin* at the graveside
before leaving. It is said that this helps the dead person when
they are questioned in the grave by the two angels, Munkar
and Nakir.

Wailing, slapping your face and tearing your clothes
as a demonstration of grief is forbidden, but not weeping
from mercy. The dead person is not harmed by his family
weeping for him.

The Prophet Muhammad, may Allah bless him and
grant him peace, said, "The deceased is tortured for
the wailing of his relatives over him." He cursed those
who wail as well as those who listen to them: "Whoever strikes their own faces, tears their clothes, and
follows the ways and traditions of the pagan days of
ignorance is not of us."

The Prophet, may Allah bless him and grant him
peace, said, "Allah loves silence at three times: when
the Qur'an is recited, when an attack is launched
against the enemy, and at funerals."

It is recommended to console those experiencing loss
and to encourage them to be patient; it is also recommended
to prepare food for the family of the deceased.

If for any reason a Muslim has been buried without
having been washed and shrouded then the body should not
be dug up for this to be done if it will have already begun to

decompose. If the body has not begun to decompose, then some say that it is permissible to exhume the body, wash and shroud it, do the funeral prayer and then bury it again. Others say that it should be left as it is.

If a Muslim dies at sea, his body should be washed and shrouded and prayed over. If there is a likelihood that land will be reached before the body begins to decompose, then the deceased should be buried once the ship has landed. If land is far off, or if it is feared that the body will decompose, then the dead person is shrouded and lowered into the sea on his right side facing *qibla*. There is disagreement as to whether or not the body should be weighted down.

A Muslim should not wash his father if he is not a Muslim, nor should he put him in his grave, unless he is afraid that the body will not be buried, in which case he should cover the body and then bury it. The same applies to a mother who is not a Muslim.

The Grave

It is recommended, but not necessary, that a slight mound be made on the top of the grave. It is disliked to cover the grave in whitewash, or to place stones or wood on the grave, or to have writing on or over the grave – unless it is feared that otherwise the location of the grave will be forgotten. It is *haram* to decorate the grave just for the sake of adornment, or to erect a building over it.

The Will

After a dead Muslim has been washed, shrouded, prayed over and buried, it is necessary to share out the wealth that he or she has left behind, in accordance with the *Shari'a*.

The Prophet Muhammad said, may Allah bless him and grant him peace, "It is the duty of a Muslim who has something to be given as a bequest not to spend two nights without making a Will about it."

The basic principles that govern the distribution of a dead person's wealth are simple:

When a person dies, first of all there is taken from his capital what is necessary for shrouding and burying him, and then debts in order of merit and then whatever bequests he has made up to a third of his estate, and then the rest is inherited in fixed shares in accordance with the *Shari'a*.

Bequests can be made, for example, to relatives – including children – who are not entitled to a fixed share under the *Shari'a*, to friends or people in need who are not relatives, for public welfare, for the maintenance of mosques and places of worship, and for the upkeep of animals. Bequests can be made by a Muslim to a non-Muslim. If a Muslim dies, leaving a non-Muslim wife, she is not entitled to a fixed share, but she can be left a bequest in her husband's will. It is also said that the amount of her bequest cannot be more than the amount of the fixed share which her Muslim co-wives will inherit in accordance with the *Shari'a*. If she is the only wife, her husband can leave her a full third of his wealth.

Bequests cannot be made in favour of an heir who is already entitled to a fixed share in accordance with the *Shari'a*.

If it turns out that a person has bequeathed more than a third of his estate in his will – that is, more than he is entitled to bequeath under the *Shari'a* – then the bequests are reduced proportionally so that they no longer exceed a third of his estate in total, *unless*, that is, all the heirs who are entitled to fixed shares in accordance with the *Shari'a* agree to accept lesser shares so that all the bequests including those which exceed the third can be distributed.

A Will can be oral or written, but a written Will is better. There should be two witnesses to the Will. Once a Muslim has reached puberty, he or she can both make a Will and directly inherit under a Will. Anyone entitled to inherit before reaching puberty will have his or her inheritance looked after by a close relative or friend until puberty is reached. A bequest in a Will made during a Muslim's final illness, or a gift made shortly before and in anticipation of death, is not valid. Instead, and after he or she has died, any such bequest will not be made, and any such gift must be returned, to be included in the shares of those relatives entitled to a fixed share in accordance with the *Shari'a*.

Debts

It is very important to leave this world without being in debt, since outstanding debts incurred in this world hold a person back in the Next World. If a person dies in debt, and the wealth that he or she leaves behind is not sufficient to repay their debts, then one of the kindest things those who are still alive can do is to pay off the deceased's debts on his or her behalf.

> The Prophet Muhammad, may Allah bless him and grant him peace, said, "The soul of the believer is detained by his debts," and, "By Allah, in Whose hand is my very soul, even if a man who had outstanding debts were killed in the way of Allah, then were raised from the dead to be killed again in the way of Allah, then were raised from the dead and were killed again – he still would not enter Paradise until his debts had been paid."

The Heirs

There are five different relationships by virtue of which someone is entitled to inherit from a dead Muslim's estate: kinship, marriage, *wala'* of emancipation, slavedom and – where there is no living person entitled to inherit from the deceased – the *Bayt al-Mal*.

Only some relatives, by virtue of their relationship to the deceased – whether because of blood-ties or through marriage – are automatically entitled to inherit fixed shares under the *Shari'a*:

There are fifteen kinds of male relatives who are entitled to a fixed share: the son, the grandson (however distant), the father, the grandfather (however distant), the full brother, the half-brother by the father, the half-brother by the mother, the son of the full brother, the son of the half-brother by the father, the full paternal uncle, the son of the full paternal uncle, and the son of the paternal uncle of the father, the husband, and the male *mawla*.

There are ten kinds of female relatives who are entitled to a fixed share: the daughter, the daughter of the daughter (however distant), the mother, the grandmother by the mother, the grandmother by the father, the full sister, the half-sister by the father, the half-sister by the mother, the wife, and the female *mawla*.

'Ali ibn Abi Talib, 'AbdAllah ibn Mas'ud, Abu Hanifa and Ibn Hanbal also include the following fourteen kinds of maternal relatives, who can only inherit in certain circumstances: the children of daughters, the sons of sisters, the daughters of the brother, the daughters of the maternal and paternal uncles and their children, the maternal grandmother, the paternal uncle of the mother, the son of the brother by the mother, and the daughter of the paternal uncle. They agree that maternal relatives in this category do not inherit at all if there are paternal relatives present amongst those who are entitled to a share – unless there is a residue.

The heirs who are entitled to inherit do so either because they have been assigned a fixed share in the Qur'an or by virtue of male kinship. Whoever is entitled to a fixed share takes his share and does not exceed it. If there is only one male relative, he takes all the property. If there are others who are entitled to fixed shares as well, then he is only entitled to what is left after he and they have received their fixed shares. If there is no residue after he and they have received their fixed shares, then he does not receive anything more than that.

In this situation, there are four categories of heir:

1. Heirs who are only entitled to inherit a fixed share. There are six people who come under this category: the father, the grandmother, the husband, the wife, the half-brother by the mother and the half-sister by the mother.

2. Heirs who are only entitled to inherit by virtue of male kinship. There are nine people who come under this category: the son, the grandson, the full brother and the half-brother by the father, the paternal uncle, the son of the brother, the son of the paternal uncle, and the male and female *mawla*.

3. Heirs who inherit in accordance with both of these criteria combined. There are two people who come under this category: the father and the grandfather. Each inherits his fixed share, and then if there is any residue after any other fixed shares have been apportioned, each is entitled to a share of it by virtue of male kinship.

4. Heirs who can inherit in accordance with either of these criteria, but not both combined. There are four people who come under this category, among females: the daughter, the daughter of the son, the full sister and the half-sister by the father. If there is also a male as well in each of these female categories, and she is entitled to inherit as well as him by virtue of male kinship, then the male receives twice as much as the female. If there is no male as well, then she is entitled to inherit her fixed share as well as the full sisters. The father has kinship with the daughters.

The Shares

When the instructions in a Will are being carried out, priority is given to bequests concerning a *mawla* and a *mudabbar* – provided that any agreement concerning this was made while the testator was in good health rather than when he was ill, as is the case with all bequests – even over the payment of *zakat* which the testator had neglected to pay during his lifetime, but ordered to be paid, and which is paid out from the third of the estate. If what remains of the third of the estate after this is not enough, then everyone entitled to receive a share receives a reduced share in proportion.

The inheritance of a husband upon the death of his wife, if she has no living children or grandchildren, will be one half of the estate. If she has left any children or grandchildren, then his share will be one quarter of the estate.

The inheritance of a wife upon the death of her husband, if he has no living children or grandchildren, will be one quarter of the estate. If he has left any children or grandchildren, then her share will be one eighth of the estate.

A mother inherits one third of the estate from her son if he does not have any living children, or grandchildren, or two or more siblings. However, there are two exceptions:

1. If he is survived by a wife and both his parents. The wife receives one quarter of the estate, the mother receives one third of what is left, and the rest goes to the father.

2. If she is survived by her husband and both her parents. The husband receives one half of the estate, the mother one third of what is left, and the rest goes to the father. In other cases, she receives one third of the estate, except where her share is diminished by *'awl*, or where the deceased is survived by children, or grandchildren, or two or more siblings. In this case, the mother receives one sixth of the estate.

The share of a father from his child, if he was his father's only child and had no children of his own, is the entire estate. If the deceased has surviving children or grandchildren, however, then the father receives one sixth of the estate.

These are the basic principles which apply when determining who is to receive what. Clearly there are so many possible permutations of combinations of surviving relatives, especially in the case of large extended families, that it is impossible in a book of this size to describe every possible permutation and then to outline how the deceased's estate would be divided in each case after his or her death. Suffice it to say that there is absolute certainty in the guidance of Allah, and that any Muslim who has studied this aspect of the guidance of Islam in sufficient detail will be able to divide a dead person's estate with equity and certainty amongst whatever combination of surviving relatives there may be.

Part 2

Writing Your Will

If you want your wealth to be distributed after your death in accordance with the Shari'a of Islam, then you must write a Will which not only clearly expresses your wishes but which also is valid under English law.

This part of the book is only suitable for people making a will in England or Wales. It is not suitable for Scotland or Northern Ireland.

This part of the book is sold with the understanding that the publisher, author and retailer are not engaged in rendering legal services. If legal advice or other expert assistance is required, or where there is any doubt as to whether any such advice or assistance is required, then the services of a competent professional should be sought. Neither this nor any other publication can take the place of a solicitor on important legal matters.

Before writing your Will, please read carefully the explanations which follow.

Introduction

There is not a country in the world today whose rulers can claim that all its laws are in accordance with the *Shari'a* of Islam. Accordingly all Muslims living today are faced with the challenge of living in accordance with the *Shari'a* as far as they are able to do so, while realising that they will not always be able to put what they know into action. In the United Kingdom, for example, all Muslims at one time or another are obliged to submit to man-made laws which either conflict or are not in harmony with the *Shari'a* of Islam. It is, however, often possible to follow the *Shari'a* without breaking the English law, and *vice versa*. It is also possible at times to do something in accordance with the *Shari'a* by *utilising* the English law, rather than by trying to avoid it. Writing a valid Will which will be recognised by the English courts, even though it expresses the deceased's wish to have his or her wealth distributed in accordance with the *Shari'a*, is one example of this – even though many of the principles governing the English law of inheritance are different from the criteria which are applied within the *Shari'a*. For example:

• If you do not leave a valid Will, then under English law you are deemed to have died 'intestate', and your wealth will be distributed to certain relatives in fixed shares – which are not the same as those laid down by the *Shari'a* – or if there are no such relatives, then it will go to the Crown: that is, the government.

• If you are married, and if both you and your spouse die leaving children under 18 years old, and if there is no valid Will stating whom you would like to be the guardian of any minor children who survive you, then they would most probably be taken into care by the Local Authority.

• If you have been married only in accordance with the *Shari'a* in the United Kingdom, you will not be regarded as having been legally married for the purposes of English law. This means that if you die without having made a Will, your spouse will be regarded as an 'unmarried partner' and would not be permitted to inherit anything from your estate.

• If, on the other hand, you married both under the *Shari'a* and under English law at a registry office, and were then subsequently divorced under the *Shari'a* but not under English law, then under English law you would still be regarded as 'married', and if you then died without having made a Will, your former spouse would then inherit from your estate even though he or she would no longer be entitled to a fixed share under the *Shari'a*. If you were also in the process of being divorced under English law, but the decree absolute had not yet been pronounced at the time of your death, then again, under English law you would still be regarded as legally 'married'.

• Similarly, if a Muslim man married a non-Muslim woman both under the *Shari'a* and under English law at a registry office, and then he died without leaving a Will, then under English law she would be regarded as his married partner and accordingly entitled to a certain share of his property, whereas under the *Shari'a* she would not be entitled to a fixed share of his property – although he would have been entitled to make a specific bequest to her out of a third of his property, provided that it did not exceed the fixed share that she would have received had she been a Muslim.

• In other words, there are contradictions between the English law and the *Shari'a*. When each is applied separately to an identical situation, the outcome is different, depending on which set of criteria is applied – although of course there are times when there is an overlap between the two and some of the criteria are identical.

• Since English law is at present not subject to the *Shari'a*, and is inevitably regarded in the English courts as having precedence over the *Shari'a*, it follows that where there is any apparent contradiction between the two, the English law will always be applied. This means, in practical terms, that it is necessary to comply with all the legal formalities required by English law before a Will can be regarded as valid. Provided that this is done, the English courts will then be prepared to give effect to your intentions as expressed in your Will – including having your property distributed in accordance with the *Shari'a* after your death – provided that these intentions are clearly expressed and are free from ambiguity.

• In other words, it is possible, under English law, to prepare a valid Will stating that you wish your wealth to be distributed in accordance with the *Shari'a* of Islam, and so to subsequently have your wealth distributed in this manner after your death, *provided that* you have complied with all the legal formalities required by English law. In order to do this, it is necessary to have an understanding of both the *Shari'a* and English law, since both require certain conditions to be fulfilled. Thus, for example, if the requirements under English law are not fulfilled, then your Will will not be considered valid; and if these requirements have been satisfied and your Will is valid, then you must also have ensured that the wishes expressed in your Will are in accordance with the *Shari'a*.

• So in order to ensure that your assets are distributed in accordance with the *Shari'a* after your death, you *must* write a Will, and that Will *must* comply with the requirements of English law in order to be valid. If you do not do this, your wealth will not be distributed in accordance with the *Shari'a* after you die. The main requirements, of both the *Shari'a* and English law, are as follows.

Under the Shari'a

- Please read the appropriate sections in Part One (on pages 24 to 30) as well as the following.

- Your Will can be either verbal or written, but there must be two witnesses to it. It is better to have a written Will, since this is more certain and capable of verification. A child who has reached puberty is capable of both making a Will and directly inheriting property from someone who has died.

- You are free to leave up to *one third* of your wealth – after any debts and expenses have been paid – to whomever you wish, but the remaining *two thirds* must be distributed among your surviving relatives in fixed shares.

- If, however, you do leave what turns out to be *more* than one third of your wealth, then these bequests may still be distributed as stipulated *provided that* all those who are entitled to fixed shares from the two thirds agree to this and accordingly to accept a corresponding reduction in their shares. If they do not agree to this, then the bequests regarding the *one third* will be reduced proportionally, so that they no longer exceed one third in total.

- If you do not write a Will, then your wealth will be automatically distributed amongst those surviving relatives who are entitled to fixed shares in accordance with the *Shari'a* – or if there are none, then it will automatically go to the *Bayt al-Mal*. As already pointed out, however, this is not the case in any country where the dominant law is not the *Shari'a*. So even if you do not wish to make any specific bequests, and simply want the automatic distribution to take place after your death, then in the United Kingdom you must nevertheless write a valid Will stating that this is what you want to happen.

The One Third

• As regards the *one third* of your wealth, it is important to remember that none of this may be left to any relative who will already be receiving a fixed share of the remaining *two thirds* in accordance with the *Shari'a*.

• It is permissible to leave all or part of the *one third* to someone who is not a Muslim. (It is also permissible to inherit *from* someone who is not a Muslim, *provided that* this is by means of a specific bequest made in the dead person's Will, rather than as a result of the operation of the English law of intestacy.)

• As well as any taxes or debts that may have to be paid after your death, it is also important to bear in mind that some additional expenses may be incurred – including funeral expenses and expenses arising out of the administration of your estate after your death – and accordingly if you do wish to bequeath up to one third of your wealth, then these expenses should first be taken into account when assessing how much that one third is likely to be.

The Two Thirds

• As regards the *two thirds* of your wealth, it is permissible to state in your Will that certain items should go to certain relatives, *provided that* the value of any such items does not exceed the value of the particular fixed share to which any such relative is entitled under the *Shari'a*.

• If, however, a particular item is worth more than a person's share, it may still go to him or her *provided that* all the other inheritors agree to this, and accordingly to accept a corresponding reduction in their shares.

- If you do not bequeath all or any of the *one third* of your wealth, then whatever has not been bequeathed by you will also be distributed among your surviving relatives in the fixed shares laid down by the *Shariʻa*.

Marriage and Divorce

- If you marry under the *Shariʻa* and then subsequently die, your new spouse will automatically be entitled to a fixed share on your death in accordance with the *Shariʻa*.

- If you are married at the time of your death to more than one and up to four wives under the *Shariʻa*, then they will all be equally entitled to fixed shares of your estate in accordance with the *Shariʻa*.

- If you have recently divorced, and one of you then dies, the one who is left will still be entitled to a fixed share in accordance with the *Shariʻa provided that* the woman is still in her *ʻidda* period. If the *ʻidda* period has been completed prior to your death, then the surviving former spouse is no longer automatically entitled to a fixed share. However, if you wish you can still leave him or her something out of the *one third* which can be left to anyone, provided that this is stipulated in your will.

Minors and Guardians

- As already stated, a child cannot directly inherit property until he or she has reached puberty. Any child who inherits property before reaching puberty will have it looked after by a guardian appointed from amongst the deceased's surviving relatives or close friends.

• Where a Muslim man dies leaving a pregnant wife, his estate is not distributed until either a child is born or there is a miscarriage or stillbirth. Once the outcome of the pregnancy is known for certain, then the distribution of the deceased's estate takes place, with any child of his born after his death receiving his or her share in accordance with the *Shari'a*.

• Guardians who look after children and their property until they reach puberty are warned in the Qur'an to behave correctly, since ultimately they will have to answer for their actions to Allah.

No Surviving Relatives

• If you have no surviving relatives who would have been entitled to fixed shares if they had survived you, then you may still leave up to *one third* of your wealth to whomever you wish, but the remaining *two thirds* will go to the *bayt al-mal* of your community, from which it will eventually be distributed amongst people in your community who are in need.

• Unlike *zakat* – which can only be distributed amongst certain categories of people – wealth such as this coming into the *bayt al-mal* can be distributed by the leader of the community as he considers best, provided of course that any such distribution is in accordance with the Shari'a.

• In this case, and if at present the *bayt al-mal* of your community is administered by means of a charitable trust under English law, then you should end your Will by making what is called a 'residuary gift' to that charitable trust. Under English law, the residuary gift is comprised of whatever may be left of your estate when all debts, taxes, expenses and other specific bequests have been paid out. The person or institution to whom the residuary gift is left is called the 'residuary legatee', since he or she or it will receive the residuary – that is, whatever is left over.

• Under English law, if there is no residuary legatee, and if you have no surviving relatives, then under the law of intestacy, any residue will go to the Crown.

• Fortunately, this situation should not arise, whether or not you have surviving relatives, *provided that* you have stated in your Will that you wish your wealth to be distributed in accordance with the *Shari'a*, since under the *Shari'a* whatever remains – after all debts, taxes and expenses have been paid, and after any gifts of up to *one third* of your remaining wealth have been made – will either be divided amongst your surviving relatives in fixed shares, or if there are none, then it will automatically go to the *Bayt al-Mal* of your community.

• Nevertheless, it is wise, for the purposes of English law, to make a residuary gift in your Will, just in case you have no surviving relatives for whatever reason at the time of your death and just in case it is not clear who is in charge of the *Bayt al-Mal* of your community. Perhaps, for example, there is more than one charitable trust in your community which all share in fulfilling the functions of the *Bayt al-Mal*. By making at least one of those charitable trusts your residuary legatee, your intention will be clear and free from ambiguity. Alternatively, since under English law your residuary gift can be given to any number of beneficiaries, you can name all or some of the charitable trusts functioning in your community as your residuary legatees; but in this case you must state the share of the residue which each trust is to receive, whether equal or otherwise.

• If at the time of your death there are no charitable trusts fulfilling the functions of the *bayt al-mal* in your community, and if it is not clear who is in charge of the *bayt al-mal* in your community – and in order to avoid any possibility of the English courts declaring that the residuary gift in your Will is invalid because of lack of certainty and is therefore to be distributed in accordance with the English law of intestacy – the attached Will form specifically provides that in the event of your residuary gift to the *bayt al-mal* failing for any reason, then the executors of your Will are to hold any residue of your estate on trust and to distribute it amongst those in need amongst your community as they in their absolute discretion consider and think fit.

• Finally, since there are slight variations between the four *madhdhabs*, you should state clearly in your Will which *madhdhab's fiqh* should be applied when your wealth is distributed. Provision is made for this in the attached Will form.

Under English Law

• You must be at least 18 years old and of sound mind before you can make a valid Will – which must be in writing – or before you can directly inherit property under someone else's Will.

• Thus although, for example, a Muslim youth aged 17 could write a Will which would be regarded as valid under the *Shari'a* (provided that all the relevant requirements under the *Shari'a* were met), this Will would never be regarded as a valid Will under English law (unless the youth was a member of Her Majesty's armed forces on active duty), and so his property would not be distributed in accordance with his Will, whatever his age when he died.

• Similarly, although a Muslim youth aged 17 could be directly given any wealth or property that had been left to him under someone's Will, under English law it would have to be held on trust for him until he had reached the age of 18 – or, if the Will specified a different age such as 21 or 25, until he had reached that age.

• As regards other basic requirements under English law, there should be no corrections or amendments in the wording of your Will *unless* these have been signed and dated by yourself and by both witnesses to the Will. Accordingly it is better to prepare a rough draft of your Will and then to write out your Will word perfect once you know exactly what you are going to write. You should make sure that your Will is expressed in simple straight forward language which makes your intentions clear, and that any items and people mentioned in your Will are correctly and clearly identified and named, and that any addresses given are accurate and up to date.

• Once your Will is finalised and completed, make sure that you destroy any draft Wills that you have prepared, as well as any earlier Wills – including copies – which you may have made in the past, in order to avoid any confusion.

Gifts and Residuary Gifts

• Subject to any debts, taxes and expenses which must first be paid out from your estate, and subject to certain restrictions as regards making children – who have not yet been born at the time of your death – beneficiaries under your Will, you can leave whatever you wish to whomever you wish. Gifts of items or property are usually called bequests. Gifts of money are usually called legacies.

• As already mentioned, it is always wise to make a residuary gift in your Will in order to avoid the possibility of dying partially intestate. In other words, if there is a residue which has not been left to anyone under the terms of your Will, then it will be distributed in accordance with the English law of intestacy – which may result in a distribution which you may not have wanted, and which is not in accordance with the *Shari‘a*.

• As already explained, under English law the residuary gift is comprised of whatever may be left of your wealth after all debts, taxes, expenses and other specific bequests have been paid out. The person or institution to whom the residuary gift is left is called the 'residuary legatee', since he or she or it will receive the residuary – whatever is left.

• Since there is always the possibility that your residuary legatee may cease to exist just before or very soon after you, it is also wise to name any alternative residuary beneficiary whom you would like to inherit in such a situation.

Witnesses

• Your Will is not valid until you have signed it and dated it in the presence of two witnesses who must then also sign the Will in your presence. The witnesses *must not* be beneficiaries under your Will, nor can they be the husband or wife of any beneficiary under your Will. In other words your witnesses must be people who will not receive anything of your wealth under the terms of your Will after you have died. Their correct addresses, as well as their full names and occupations, must be included in the Will.

• If you do choose a beneficiary, or any beneficiary's wife or husband, as a witness then they will not be permitted to benefit from your Will – although the rest of the Will will be regarded as valid. Although it is not necessary, it is better – in case anyone subsequently disputes the validity of your Will – for any witness to be *at least* 18 years old, and preferably neither very old nor hard to trace.

• Once your Will has been signed and witnessed, put it in a safe place and make sure that your executors know exactly where it is being kept so that when you die they will know where to find it. This is also important if your Will contains directions concerning where you want to be buried, and the kind of funeral which you wish to have. As well as having a clause dealing with this, the attached Will form also states, in accordance with the teachings of Islam, that you do not wish to have your body subjected to a *post mortem*, or to have any of your organs used for transplants or medical research.

• It will also help your executors if you leave – with, but not in, your Will – details of where any important documents are being kept, where any property that you own is located, and who should be notified of your death.

Formalities between Death and Burial

• Unfortunately the authorities do sometimes insist that a *post mortem* be carried out on the dead body – usually where death has occurred in sudden or suspicious circumstances – in which case there is little that can be done to prevent it, even though this practice is contrary to the teachings of Islam.

• Where, however, the cause of death is both clear and natural – for example, someone who dies of a terminal illness for which he or she had been receiving treatment during the months leading up to the moment of death – then a 'routine' *post mortem* can be avoided.

• Although, in accordance with the *Sunna*, a person who has just died should be washed, shrouded, prayed over and buried as soon as possible, under English law a dead body cannot be buried until a death certificate has been issued.

• An initial medical death certificate is usually issued by the hospital authorities or the General Practitioner in attendance where death occurs at home. In the case of sudden death, this is only issued once the *post mortem* has been carried out. The certificate, which is given to the closest relative or known executor, has to be sent or taken to the Registrar of Births, Deaths and Marriages within five days. That Registrar will then issue the formal death certificate, after which the body can be buried.

• There are a growing number of graveyards for Muslims in the United Kingdom, and the necessary arrangements to have a grave dug and the body buried can be made with the local authority responsible for the Muslim cemetery in which the body is to be buried.

• If there is no Muslim cemetery near your community, your representatives should approach your local authority to arrange for one, preferably at a location where all the graves will be aligned with *qibla* (in the United Kingdom this is 127 degrees south-east). The Community Relations Commission has prepared specific guidance for local authorities in helping to meet this need, and if approached with courtesy most local authorities will help, particularly if the Muslim community is prepared to contribute towards the cost of landscaping the site and planting a hedge or shrubs round its borders.

Executors

• After your death and burial, your Will is administered by people known as executors, who have to obtain what are called 'letters of probate' from the court, whereby the validity of the Will is confirmed and the executors are given the authority to manage your estate, before they can deal with your estate and distribute your wealth in accordance with your wishes. If you have not named any executors in your Will, then the court will choose administrators to deal with your estate – who are likely to be close members of your family – but this may well involve delay and expense, which will be paid out from your estate.

• So it is better to choose your executors before you die, to make sure that they are willing to act as your executors, and to name them in your Will, together with their full names and correct addresses.

• Your executors – who *must* be *at least* 18 years old – *may* be chosen from amongst those people who will inherit from you under the terms of your Will, but if so, they must not also be either of the two witnesses to the Will – because if this is the case, then as already explained they will not be allowed to inherit anything under the Will. It is usual to choose two executors – especially if there are any children who may benefit from the Will *before* they are 18 years old, in which case the executors will hold any minor's share on trust until they reach the age of 18 – but otherwise it is sufficient to have just one executor, especially if you are not wealthy and your Will is simple. It is always wise to name a third person whom you would like to act as your executor just in case either or both of your named executors are unable to act as such for whatever reason after your death. Provision for this is made in the attached Will form.

• Since not many Muslims are familiar with how a dead person's property should be divided in accordance with the *Shari'a*, it would help with the administration of your estate after your death if at least one of your executors either has this knowledge or already knows of someone who has this knowledge and who would be able to assist in ascertaining which relatives are entitled to what, when the time comes to share out whatever wealth you have left behind.

Marriage and Divorce

• As has already been pointed out in the Introduction, neither marriage nor divorce conducted under the *Shari'a* in the United Kingdom are regarded as legally valid under English law. *However*, a marriage or divorce conducted in a country where the law of the land *is* the *Shari'a* – at least in these two respects, if not in others – will be regarded as legally valid in England and Wales. In other words, if a marriage or divorce under the *Shari'a* is conducted in a country where such a marriage or divorce is regarded as legally valid, then the English courts will also recognise such a marriage or divorce as legally valid in England and Wales.

• It is important to remember that although it is not a criminal offence under English law to commit adultery or to have as many lovers as you wish, it is a criminal offence – called bigamy – to be married in accordance with English law with more than one spouse at the same time, even if you cherish and provide for them both. Any such second marriage contracted by either spouse of a subsisting marriage will automatically be regarded as null and void – which means that the 'second' wife or husband will be regarded as an 'unmarried partner'. Accordingly, if there is no valid Will which makes a specific bequest to him or her, he or she will not be entitled to inherit in accordance with the English law of intestacy .

• Since a marriage conducted in the United Kingdom under the *Shari'a* is not regarded as a valid marriage by English law, any Muslim man who wishes, under the *Shari'a*, to have more than one and up to four wives at any one time, is free to do so without being charged with bigamy, *provided that* he does not also marry more than one of them in accordance with English law – although of course he would be free to marry just one of them under English law as well as under the *Shari'a*, should both parties wish to do so. This means, however, that a Muslim man in this situation *must* make a valid Will if all of his wives are to inherit from him.

• If you marry someone under English law after making your Will, then that Will *automatically becomes invalid*. You should, therefore, make a new Will after your marriage, unless the pre-marriage Will states that it is being made in contemplation of your future marriage with that person (who must be specifically named), in which case there is no need to write a new Will.

• If you only marry under the *Shari'a* after making your Will, then because the English law does not regard this as a valid marriage, your Will does *not* become automatically invalid; it will remain valid.

• If at the time of your death you have more than one and up to four wives whom you married under the *Shari'a*, then – *provided that* you have left a valid Will stating that you wish your estate to be distributed in accordance with the *Shari'a* of Islam – they will all receive the fixed share of your wealth to which they are entitled.

• It should be noted that a divorce under English law does not make a Will invalid. However if your former spouse is named as a beneficiary in that Will, then he or she will not be allowed to inherit anything under that Will unless the Will expressly provides that he or she should receive a gift even after divorce. Similarly, if your former spouse is named as an executor in your Will, then after divorce he or she will not be allowed to act as your executor. In other words, if you divorce under English law after making a Will, then it is better to destroy that Will and write a new Will.

• If you only divorce under the *Shari'a*, then because the English law does not regard this as a valid divorce, the above will not apply. Nevertheless, if you have divorced only under the *Shari'a*, then it would still be wise to make a new Will for the reasons already given in the Introduction.

Minors and Guardians

• If you have any children under 18 years old, then it is wise to name a guardian to care for them in the event of their being left without either parent to look after them while they are still minors, since otherwise they might be taken into care by the local authorities. The guardian can also be one of your executors. If you and the other parent have divorced, or if there is a Court Order determining where any such child is to live or who is to have parental responsibility – or if either of these situations arise after your Will has been made – then it may not be so easy to appoint a guardian, and it would be wise to consult a solicitor before writing a Will.

• Since a child under 18 years old cannot, under English law, legally hold property that is left to him or her under a Will, the property will instead be held on trust for the child until he or she reaches the age of 18 – or a later age if so specified in the Will.

• Under English law, your trustees will have the power to advance up to half of the capital of any such child's inheritance, or to use the capital for the child's benefit, but only if they think there are good reasons for doing so. While the child is under 18, the trustees have a discretion to use the income from the inheritance for the child's maintenance, education and benefit, or to accumulate the income by adding it to the capital. The child has the right to all the *income* from the inheritance after reaching 18, whether or not you specified a greater age for taking the *capital* outright.

• In the attached Will form, the trustees have been given the power – in accordance with the *Shari'a* – to retain or sell any such property and to invest the proceeds thereof (provided that any such investment does not involve any form of usury and is permitted by the *Shari'a*), and while any such child is a minor to use all or any part of the proceeds from any such sale or the income from any such investment from the child's fixed share for the child's maintenance, education or benefit.

- In the Qur'an, Allah warns trustees and guardians in this position to deal fairly and honestly with any wealth which they hold on trust for a minor.

Joint Ownership of Property

- If you jointly own property, then it will be held either under a 'joint tenancy' or under a 'tenancy in common'. If the property is held under a joint tenancy, then when you die your interest in the property *automatically* goes to your surviving co-owner. If your property is owned under a tenancy in common, however, then you can leave your share under the terms of your will.

- If you wish to change a joint tenancy into a tenancy in common, you must do so by giving your co-owner written notice of your intention *before* your death, and not in your Will.

- If you wish to change a tenancy in common into a joint tenancy, you should see a solicitor.

- Although taking out a mortgage is clearly a *haram* transaction, many Muslims today have done so. It is almost impossible to distribute a Muslim's wealth in accordance with the *Shari'a* where he or she dies with an outstanding mortgage, especially if it is a joint mortgage. Not only do the surviving relatives inherit a *haram* debt, but also – in the case of a joint mortgage – the right to possession of the property together with the obligation to pay off the mortgage, usually automatically passes to the survivor under the terms of the mortgage – whereas, under the *Shari'a*, if there are other surviving relatives, they would probably be entitled to a share in the property.

• If the deceased also left enough money to repay the mortgage, then it is possible to treat the mortgage as an outstanding debt which is to be repaid in full before division of the estate takes place. If you are in a position to do this, you should stipulate this in your Will by stating that you leave the house to so and so 'free from all encumbrances'.

• If you are not going to be able to leave enough money to repay the mortgage out of your estate after your death, then you will have to bequeath the property 'subject to the mortgage on it'. In that case the property can only be eventually shared between surviving relatives in accordance with the *Shari'a either* by selling the property, repaying the mortgage and dividing whatever is left in accordance with the *Shari'a, or* – where the surviving mortgagee wishes to remain in possession of the house – by calculating the value of the shares to which the surviving relatives are entitled under the *Shari'a*, and then 'buying' their shares from them.

• Both of the above solutions are unsatisfactory. It is better to free yourself of any *haram* transactions into which you may have entered before you die. The *Shari'a* can only really be applied to the distribution of your wealth after your death if you acquired it within the *Shari'a* before your death.

Changing Your Will

• If your situation changes – for example if you marry, or divorce, or dispose of or acquire possessions which are or are not referred to in your existing Will, or if you wish to change your intended beneficiaries – and so you wish to change your Will, then it is better to write a new Will and *destroy* the old one.

- Alternatively – if, for example, your existing Will is a detailed one and the proposed changes or additions are relatively minor ones – you can prepare what is called a 'codicil' which is to be read in conjunction with your main existing Will. However, if you wish to adopt this approach, it would be better to seek the assistance of a solicitor.

Taxes

- If your financial affairs are complicated, or if you are wealthy (with an estate worth more than £154,000[*], and if you have made gifts totalling more than £3,000[*] per year during the seven years before your death), then it would probably be wise to consult a Muslim solicitor who is familiar with both the *Shari'a* and the English law, in order to ensure not only that the terms of your Will are both valid and in accordance with your wishes, but also that your estate will not be subject to any more taxes – such as income tax, capital gains tax and inheritance tax – than is absolutely necessary. In this case it would also be wise to make the same solicitor (or the firm of solicitors to which he or she belongs) one of your executors.

- The Prophet Muhammad, may Allah bless him and grant him peace, demonstrated the best way of leaving this world – which was virtually the same way as he entered it, possessing nothing and owing nothing.

- [*] N.B. These figures are accurate as at 1st May 1995, but may be subject to change by the government. There is no inheritance tax liability on anything given to your spouse.

- *Please read the following instructions carefully before making your Will.*

Instructions

- Your Will should be typewritten or written in ink – *not* pencil.

- Remember, there should be no crossings out or alterations in your Will.

- Before writing your Will, prepare a draft Will. It may help to first prepare a list of everything that belongs to you, so that you can decide, subject to the *Shari'a*, who should be receiving what. Remember that anything of yours which you do not specifically bequeath to a named person will either be divided amongst your surviving relatives in accordance with the *Shari'a* or, in the absence of any such relatives, it will go to the *Bayt al-Mal* of your community or to whoever has been named as the residuary beneficiary or beneficiaries.

- It is important to ensure that your Will is expressed in simple straightforward language that makes your intentions clear. Make sure that any items and people mentioned in your Will are correctly and clearly identified and named, and that any addresses given are accurate and up to date.

- In order to avoid any possibility of forgery by someone else, you should not leave any large gaps or spaces between items or paragraphs. If any section is not applicable, write 'not applicable'. If some space is left at the end of a section, especially in sections 8 and 9, then draw a line through it, so that nothing else can be added.

- Remember to sign and date your Will immediately under the bottom line of your Will – in the *presence* of your two witnesses – and to ensure that the two witnesses then sign their names – in *your presence* – under the attestation clause, as well as writing down their addresses and occupations.

• The two witnesses do not have to read the contents of your Will, since their only duty is to confirm your signature.

• Do not staple, pin or otherwise attach any other document to your Will.

• Keep your Will in a safe place and make sure that your executors know where it is. If you wish, you can deposit it at the Probate Registry. If you want to keep a photocopy in case the original is lost or destroyed, mark it clearly as such.

• It would also help those who are going to conclude your affairs after your death if you leave details of what your funeral wishes are, where any important documents are being kept, where any property that you own is located, and who should be notified of your death.

• It is worth remembering that after you have written your Will, you are still free to deal with your assets as you wish, including selling or otherwise disposing of any property you may own. If, however, you sell a house which you have bequeathed to a friend in your Will, and then buy another house, and then die before having amended your Will accordingly, your friend will not receive either of these houses. In other words, if your Will eventually contains bequests that are no longer possible because you no longer possess the items, it will be time to prepare a new Will.

• *Please read the notes which accompany the attached Will form carefully before making your Will.*

Counsel on Death

Prepare yourself for death, oh my brother, for it will descend.
Do not draw out your hopes in case your heart treats you harshly.

Persevere in reflection which will make you aware
and move you to do good works, for life will depart.

Constantly go over the states of the last hour, the raising
of bodies, the gathering, and the balance which is set up.

Then there is the bridge which will have obstacles laid out
on it to make the crossing difficult for the rebellious.

While whoever was obedient and sincere towards Allah
will pass over it like a flash of lightning or a wind
and will go on.

If you wish to be given a drink from the fountain on the day
of gathering you must love the Prophet and his descendants.

And bless the guide who intercedes for mankind.
He is the one who will plead for us when creation is terrified.

May the blessings of Allah be upon him in every country,
and his family and Companions and those who love him.

I ask the Lord, Allah, for the gift of bliss
and a seal of goodness for me and those who draw near.

**(From the *Diwan* of
Shaykh Muhammad ibn al-Habib)**

Glossary of Arabic Terms

Akhira : the next world, what is on the other side of death, the world after this world in the realm of the Unseen.

'asr : the obligatory mid-afternoon prayer which can be prayed at any time between mid-afternoon and a little before sunset.

'awl : the responsibility of having to support family members, especially in a large, extended family.

aya (plural **ayat**) : a sign, a verse of the Qur'an. There are 6,666 *ayat* in the Qur'an.

Bayt al-Mal : the 'house of wealth', the treasury of the Muslims where income from *zakat* and other sources – including the wealth of Muslims who die without leaving a Will or any relatives entitled to that wealth in accordance with the *Shari'a* – is gathered for redistribution.

deen : the life-transaction, submission and obedience to a particular system of rules and practices; a debt of exchange between two parties, in this usage between the Creator and the created. Allah says in the Qur'an, '*Surely the deen with Allah is Islam.*' (3.19).

dhuhr : the obligatory mid-day prayer which can be prayed at any time between noon and mid-afternoon.

du'a : making supplication to Allah.

fajr : dawn, first light.

fard : obligatory acts as defined by the *Shari'a*. This is divided into *fard 'ayn* which is what is obligatory for every adult Muslim, and *fard kifaya* which is what is obligatory on at least one of the adults in any Muslim community. The knowledge of which relatives are entitled to what shares of a dead Muslim's wealth, for example, is *fard kifaya*.

Fatiha : 'The Opening', the opening *Sura* of the Qur'an.

fiqh : the science of the application of the *Shari'a*.

ghusl : the ritual washing of the whole body with water to be pure for the prayer. It is necessary to have a *ghusl* on embracing Islam, after sexual intercourse or seminal emission, at the end of menstruation, after childbirth, and before being buried – when your body is washed for you. It is recommended, but not obligatory, for anyone who washes a dead body to have a *ghusl* afterwards.

hadd (plural **hudood**) **:** the limits, Allah's definitions of what is *halal* and *haram*. The *hadd* punishments are the specific fixed penalties laid down by the *Shari'a* for certain specified crimes.

Hajj : the yearly pilgrimage to Makka which every Muslim who has the means and ability must make once in his or her lifetime, and the performance of the rites of the *Hajj* in and around Makka.

halal : permitted by the *Shari'a*.

haram : forbidden by the *Shari'a*; see also *Haram*.

Haram : a sacred protected area in which certain behaviour is forbidden and other behaviour obligatory. The area around the *Ka'ba* in Makka is a *Haram*, as is the area around the Prophet's Mosque, in which is the Prophet Muhammad's tomb, may Allah bless him and grant him peace, in Madina. They are referred to together as the *Haramayn*.

hasan : an adjective describing a married person, from the noun *hisn*, a fortress. Anyone who has been made *hasan* by marriage (*muhsan*) is liable to have the full *hadd* punishment of death inflicted on them if they commit adultery.

'idda : a period after divorce (3 menstrual periods), or the death of her husband (4 lunar months and 10 days), for which a woman waits before remarrying to ensure that there is no confusion about the paternity of children born after divorce or death.

ihsan : spiritual excellence; being absolutely sincere to Allah in oneself; it is to worship Allah as though you see Him, knowing that although you do not see Him, He sees you.

Imam : one who leads the prayer; an eminent scholar.

iman : acceptance, belief, trust, in Allah – a gift from Him; it is to believe in Allah, His angels, His books, His Messengers, the Last Day and the Garden and the Fire, and that everything is by the Decree of Allah, both the good and the evil.

'isha : the obligatory night prayer which can be prayed at any time between nightfall and a little before dawn.

Islam : peace and submission to the will of Allah, the way of life embodied by all the prophets, given its final form in the prophetic guidance brought by the Prophet Muhammad, may the blessings and peace of Allah be on him. The five pillars of *Islam* are the affirmation of the *shahada*, performing the *salat*, paying the *zakat*, fasting the month of *Ramadan*, and doing the *hajj* at least once in your lifetime if you are able.

janaba : the impure state in which a person requires a *ghusl* before prayer is permissible again.

jinn : unseen beings created from smokeless fire who inhabit the earth together with mankind.

Ka'ba : the cube-shaped building at the centre of the *Haram* in Makka, originally built by the Prophet Ibrahim on the site of the first place of worship built by the Prophet Adam, peace be on them, and rebuilt with the help of the Prophet Muhammad, may Allah bless him and grant him peace; also known as the House of Allah. The *Ka'ba* is the focal point which all Muslims face when doing the *salat*. This does not mean that Allah lives inside the *Ka'ba*, nor does it mean that the Muslims worship the *Ka'ba*. It is Allah Who is worshipped, and He is not contained or confined in any form or place or time or concept.

kafir (plural **kafirun** or **kuffar**) : a person who commits *kufr*, the opposite of a *mu'min*.

kitaba : a contract by which a slave acquires his freedom against a future payment or payments by instalments to his owner.

kufr : to cover up the truth, to reject Allah and His Messenger, may Allah bless him and grant him peace.

lahd : a grave, about five feet deep, in which – after digging the basic trench – a niche is dug for the body into the bottom of the side which faces *qibla*, so that the body is protected by the overhang.

Madina : the City, often called al-Madinat al-Munawwara – the illuminated, or the enlightened, city – where the revelation of the Qur'an was completed and in which the Prophet Muhammad died and is buried, may Allah bless him and grant him peace.

madhdhab : a school of *fiqh*. There are four main *madhdhabs* – the Hanafi, the Maliki, the Shafi'i and the Hanbali.

maghrib : the obligatory sunset prayer which should be prayed straight after sunset.

Makka : the city in which the *Ka'ba* stands, and in which the Prophet Muhammad was born, may Allah bless him and grant him peace, and in and around which the revelation of the Qur'an commenced.

mawla : a person with whom a tie of *wala'* has been established by manumission. It usually refers to a freed slave, but it can also mean the former master.

mudabbar : a slave who has been given a *tadbir*, a contract to be freed after his master's death.

mukatab : a slave who has been given a *kitaba*, a contract to buy his freedom.

mu'min (plural - **mu'minun**) **:** someone who possesses the quality of *iman*, who trusts in Allah and accepts His Messenger, may Allah bless him and grant him peace, and for whom the *Akhira* is more real than this world.

Munkar and Nakir : the two angels who question your *ruh* in the grave after your body has been buried, asking, "Who is your Lord? Who is your Prophet? What is your Book? What was your *Deen*?"

niyya : intention. Actions are judged by their intentions.

qabr : the grave, experienced as a place of peace and light and space by the *ruh* of the *mu'min* who sees his or her place in the Garden in the morning and in the evening; and experienced as a place of torment and darkness and no space by the *ruh* of the *kafir* who sees his or her place in the Fire in the morning and in the evening. After death there is a period of waiting in the grave for the *ruh* until the Last Day arrives, when everyone who has ever lived will be brought back to life and gathered together. Their actions and intentions will be weighed in the Balance, and everyone will either go to the Garden or to the Fire, for ever.

qibla : the direction faced in prayer, which, for the Muslims, is towards the *Ka'ba* in Makka.

Qur'an : 'the Recitation', the latest and last Revelation from Allah to mankind and the *jinn* before the end of the world. It was revealed to the Prophet Muhammad, may Allah bless him and grant him peace, through the Angel Jibril, over a period of twenty-three years, of which the first thirteen were spent in Makka, and the last ten in Madina. The Qur'an amends, encompasses, expands, surpasses and abrogates all the earlier Revelations given to the earlier Messengers, peace be on all of them. The Qur'an is the greatest miracle given to the Prophet Muhammad by Allah, for he was illiterate and could neither read nor write. The Qur'an is the uncreated Word of Allah. The Qur'an still exists today exactly as it was originally revealed, without any change or addition or deletion.

Ramadan : the sacred month of fasting and worship: the ninth month in the Muslim lunar calendar, during which all adult Muslims who are in good health fast from the first light of dawn until sunset each day.

ruh : the spirit which gives life, formed from pure light; also the Angel Jibril.

sajda : the act of prostrating oneself before Allah, particularly in the *salat*, the prayer.

salam : peace; the greeting with which the *salat* ends, *as-salamu'alaykum*, which means 'peace be on you', is usually called the *taslim*.

salat : the prayer, particularly the five daily obligatory prayers of the Muslims which are called *maghrib*, *'isha*, *subh*, *dhuhr* and *'asr*. They consist of fixed sets of standings, bowings, prostrations and sittings in worship of Allah. The

Muslim day begins at *maghrib*, because the first day of a new month is only determined when the new moon is sighted shortly after sunset.

shahada : to witness, to bear witness that there is no god except Allah and that Muhammad is the Messenger of Allah, may Allah bless him and grant him peace.

shaqq : a simple grave, about five feet deep. It sometimes has a small ledge dug around its interior about two feet up from the bottom, so that after the body has been placed in the grave, a protective layer of wood or clay slabs can be placed over the body – resting on the ledge – before the grave is filled in with earth.

Shari'a : a road, the legal and social modality of a people based on the revelation of their Prophet. The last *Shari'a* in history is that of Islam. It abrogates all previous *Shari'as*. Being the last, it is also the easiest to follow, and unlike its predecessors, it is for the whole human race, wherever they are, rather than for a particular tribe or people.

shuruq : sunrise, when the sun is fully over the horizon.

subh : the obligatory dawn prayer which can be prayed at any time between *fajr* and a short while before the sun rises.

Sunna : a form, the customary practice of a person or group of people. It has come to refer almost exclusively to the practice of the Messenger of Allah, Muhammad, may Allah bless him and grant him peace, but also comprises the customs of the first generation of Muslims in Madina – whose knowledge and behaviour were directly based on what they had observed and learned from Muhammad.

Sura : a large unit of Qur'an linked by thematic content, composed of *ayat*. There are 114 *Suras* in the Qur'an.

Surat YaSin : the 36th *Sura* in the Qur'an, often referred to as the 'heart of the Qur'an'.

tabaraka wa ta'ala : may He (Allah) be blessed and exalted.

tadbir : a contract given by a master to a slave that the slave will be freed after the master dies.

takbir : the saying of *Allahu akbar* which means 'Allah is greater'. The *salat* begins with a *takbir*.

tayammum : purification for prayer using clean dust, earth or stone, when water for *ghusl* or *wudu'* is either unavailable or would be detrimental to health. *Tayammum* is done by striking the earth or rubbing the stone with the palms of the hands and then wiping the face and hands and forearms.

wala' : the tie of clientage, established between a freed slave and the person who frees him, whereby the one who has been set free becomes integrated into the family of his or her former master.

wudu' : washing of the hands, mouth, nostrils, face, forearms, head, ears and feet with water so as to be pure for the prayer. You must already be in *ghusl* for *wudu'* to be effective.

zakat : the wealth tax obligatory on Muslims each year, usually payable in the form of one fortieth of surplus wealth which is more than a certain fixed minimum amount, called the *nisab*. *Zakat* is payable on accumulated wealth, merchandise, certain crops, certain livestock, and subterranean and mineral wealth, such as, for example, gold and oil.

Glossary of English Legal Terms

administrator : a person appointed by the Probate Registry in the absence of a Will being found – or a person who is appointed to prove a will in the event of there being no executor named in a Will – to manage the estate of a deceased. A relative or close friend of a beneficiary may be asked to administer the estate, in order of beneficial priority.

adult : under English law, a person aged 18 or over.

assets : all that you own, including money, possessions and property.

beneficiary : a person who inherits under a will, or under intestacy laws, or who receives payment from a life insurance policy or under a trust.

bequest : a gift from someone's estate other than immovable property such as a house or land.

children : this term may be used to refer to both legitimate and illegitimate children, and to children who have been legally adopted into the family, but it does not include stepchildren – who must therefore be specifically mentioned if they are to benefit under a Will.

codicil : a document made by you at a later date which makes an addition or alteration to your Will, but which does not revoke it. If certain formalities are not fulfilled, a codicil will not be regarded as valid.

deceased : the person who has died.

distribution : the process of dealing with an estate after receiving the Grant of Probate or Letters of Administration: first paying any debts, taxes and expenses, and then dividing up the remainder between the beneficiaries.

donee : a person who receives a gift.

donor : a person who gives the gift.

encumbrance : usually a mortgage or charge upon property securing the payment of a debt or other liability.

estate : the total of all the property, money and possessions belonging to a person at death.

executor : a person appointed by you in your Will to deal with the estate after your death. This person cannot charge a fee unless previously authorised by the Will, although he or she is entitled to be repaid any expenses incurred in dealing with your estate, such as, for example, the cost of making photocopies, telephone calls, postage and loss of earnings.

guardian : a person with legally authorised control and responsibility for a minor child.

immovable property : real property which cannot be moved, such as land or buildings.

inheritance tax : a tax imposed on a person's estate upon death and in some cases on gifts made during the person's lifetime where the value of the estate and/or gifts is above a certain amount.

intestate : If you die without having made a valid Will, you are said to have died intestate: your estate will be subject to the rules of intestacy and distributed accordingly.

joint property : property owned jointly with another person or persons.

joint tenant : this term is used to describe two or more people who jointly own property in undivided shares. When one joint tenant dies, that person's share automatically passes to the surviving joint tenant or tenants. Compare with *tenant in common.*

legacy : a specific gift of money (known as a pecuniary legacy) or property (known as a special legacy) other than a building or land.

legatee : the person to whom a legacy is bequeathed.

minor : under English law, a person under the age of 18.

movable property : any personal property – other than land or buildings – which can be moved.

next of kin : your closest living relative.

personal representative : the person appointed by the Probate Court to deal with your estate in a Grant of Representation. This would include an executor named by you in your Will.

post mortem : the examination and dissection of a dead body to determine the cause of death.

probate : the document issued by the Probate Court which confirms the validity of a Will and upholds the appointment of your executor or executors to manage the estate.

residue : the remainder of an estate once all debts, taxes and administration expenses have been paid and after all specific legacies and bequests have been given to the donees.

residuary beneficiary : a beneficiary who receives the residue of an estate or part of it.

residuary gift : a gift made in a Will which disposes of part or all of any residue that there may be.

rigor mortis : muscular stiffening following death, due to chemical change in the tissues.

specific gift : a gift of a particular item of property in a Will.

Glossary

substitutional beneficiary : a person designated as a beneficiary if someone else whom you have named as a beneficiary in your Will dies before you do or fails to survive you for a specified period or to reach a specified age.

survivor : any relative mentioned in the Will who is still alive at the time of the testator's death, including those who may not have been born at the time the Will was made, subject to certain limitations. For the purposes of the *Shari'a*, a deceased's wealth is distributed amongst those relatives entitled to a share who are alive at the time of the testator's death, and including any child of his or hers born after his or her death.

tenant in common : this is the other way for two or more persons to hold property jointly. Each tenant in common has his or her own specific share in the property, which forms part of the estate at the time of death and which does not automatically pass to the other surviving tenant or tenants in common, but which will pass in accordance with the Will. If a tenant in common dies intestate, however, then his or her share will pass to the surviving tenant or tenants in common. Compare with *joint tenant*.

testamentary expenses : the cost of administering a Will, such as, making photocopies, telephone calls, postage, loss of earnings and so on.

testator : a person who makes a Will.

trust : parts of an estate, or even a whole estate, administered by a trustee or trustees for the benefit of a named person or persons in accordance with a trust document.

trustee : a person nominated to deal with a trust.

Will : a legal document which sets out the wishes of the testator for the distribution of his or her estate and certain other matters including funeral and burial (or other) arrangements.

Notes to Will Form

• *The numbers of these notes correspond to the numbers in the attached Will form. Please read these notes carefully both while preparing your draft Will and when you fill in the Will form.*

1. Give your full name.

2. Give your full address.

3. This means that *this* Will is your latest Will.

4. Make sure that the person or persons whom you name have agreed to act as your executors, and insert their full names and addresses.

5. Make sure that the person or persons whom you name have agreed to act as guardians, and insert their full names and addresses.

6. This is self-explanatory, but see also under *'executor'* in the Glossary of English Legal Terms.

7. Make sure that you insert the name of the *Imam* whose *madhdhab* you follow: e.g. *Imam* Malik, or *Imam* Abu Hanifa, or *Imam* Shafi'i, or *Imam* Ibn Hanbal.

8. Clearly identify each item and the person for whom it is intended, and remember to draw a line through any unfilled space at the end so that nothing else can be added by anyone else at a later date. Make sure that the total value of the items listed in this section will not exceed the value of one third of your estate after any debts, taxes and funeral and administration expenses have been deducted.

9. Clearly identify each item and the person for whom it is intended, and remember to draw a line through any unfilled space at the end so that nothing else can be added by anyone else at a later date. Make sure that the value of any item or items which you would like a particular relative to have does not exceed the value of the share to which he or she will be entitled.

10. If you name more than one charity, then you must state what share each charity is to receive – e.g. 'in equal shares'.

11. Please specify the *age* at which the child is to fully inherit his or her share – which, under English law, must be *at least* 18, but which could, for example, be 21 or 25.

12. Please state where you would like to be buried, together with any other instructions regarding your funeral.

- ***Please sign and date your Will in the presence of your two witnesses and then watch them sign the attestation clause in your presence immediately afterwards. Insert their full names, addresses and occupations beneath their signatures. Your Will is now completed.***

- *If there is not sufficient space in the attached Will form, then you could enlarge it to A3 size with the help of a photocopier and use that.*

they in their absolute discretion think fit – so that their total value then amounts to one third of what remains of my estate – before being distributed *unless* with reference to Clause 9 herein all my surviving relatives entitled to inherit fixed shares in accordance with the *Shari'a* of Islam agree to the above specific gifts and legacies being distributed as indicated above and accordingly to accept a corresponding decrease in the amount of their own respective shares *in which case* the above specific gifts and legacies shall be distributed as indicated above.

9. **(1)** As regards the *two thirds* of what remains of my estate (after all or any funeral expenses, debts, taxes, professional and testamentary expenses and with reference to Clause 8 herein specific gifts and legacies have been paid or distributed) which must be distributed amongst my surviving relatives in fixed shares in accordance with the *Shari'a* of Islam, I would like the following specific items to go to the following relatives *provided that* the value of any such particular item or group of items does not amount to more than the value of the particular fixed share or shares to which any such item or group of items relates and to which any such relative or relatives is or are entitled in accordance with the *Shari'a* of Islam:

....

....

....

....

....

....

....

....

....

(2) In the event of the value of any of the above specific items amounting to more than the value of the particular fixed share or shares to which any such item or group of items relates and to which any such relative or relatives is or are entitled, then my executors are instead to allocate to any such relative or relatives whatever in their absolute discretion appears best to represent their particular share or shares in my estate *unless* all my surviving relatives entitled to inherit fixed shares in accordance with the *Shari'a* of Islam agree to any such specific items being allocated as indicated above and accordingly to accept a corresponding decrease in the amount of their own respective shares *in which case* the above specific items shall be allocated as indicated above.

10. In the event of there being no surviving relatives who would have been entitled to fixed shares from my estate if they had survived me, which means that any residue of my estate (after all or any funeral expenses, debts, taxes, professional and testamentary expenses and with reference to Clause 8 herein specific gifts and legacies have been paid or distributed) will in accordance with the *Shari'a* of Islam automatically go to the *Bayt al-Mal* of my community, then I give that residue to the *Bayt al-Mal* of my community and if there is or are one or more charitable trusts performing the functions of the *Bayt al-Mal* in my community, then I give that residue to:

....

....

....

but if this gift or any part of it fails for any reason *or if any other part of this Will fails for any reason* then I wish the executors of my estate to hold the residue of my estate or the part of it affected on trust and to distribute it amongst those in need amongst my community as they in their absolute discretion consider and think fit, *provided always* that any such distribution is in accordance with and guided by the *Shari'a* of Islam.

11. In the event of any of my children or other relatives being minors at the time of my death, I wish my executors to hold their fixed share or shares as determined by the *Shari'a* of Islam on trust until any such child attains the age of ... . My trustees shall be free to retain or sell any such fixed share as